**Hi, welcome to the fun way to learn about animals through 100 BIG creative coloring pages!**

Ideally suited for kids ages 1-4 as they discover the world around them. This book is intended to boost early childhood development through engaging activities that build connections with words, pictures and colors. All the custom artwork has been created by experienced designers to be the right level for kids to stimulate imagination, to allow them to build their fine motor skills and to have a load of fun and learning in the process!

**With 100 pages of illustrations, children will explore and enjoy a HUGE variety of easy to color, fun, friendly (and sometimes silly!) animals.**

Thank you for purchasing this book and we hope you and your little ones unlock a world of coloring fun and learning! We're still learning and growing ourselves, so we'd really appreciate a review on Amazon for this book if you have time. **Thank you.**

**Check out other titles in our TODDLER COLORING series!**

ISBN: 979-8552067565     ISBN: 979-8520557715

This ANIMALS Toddler COLORING BOOK

BELONGS TO

..................................................................................

ANT

RACOON

# SHEEP

# HEDGEHOG

RAINY DAY **DUCK**

# JELLYFISH

FITNESS PANDA

# PLATYPUS

# STINGRAY

# CHAMELEON

# DRIVER BEAR

BEAR 1

GORILLA

FLAMINGO

BEAVER

# PANDA
## PARTY!

# NARWHAL

# 3 LITTLE PIGS

# SNAKE

# DINO TRICERATOPS !

# WARTHOG

# DRAGONFLY

# PILOT MOUSE

# LION

# PUFFER FISH

LADYBUG

BAT

# GRASSHOPPER

# HIPPO

# PARROT

# PUPPY

MY NAME IS ...........................

# CATERPILLAR

ELEPHANT

# CRAB

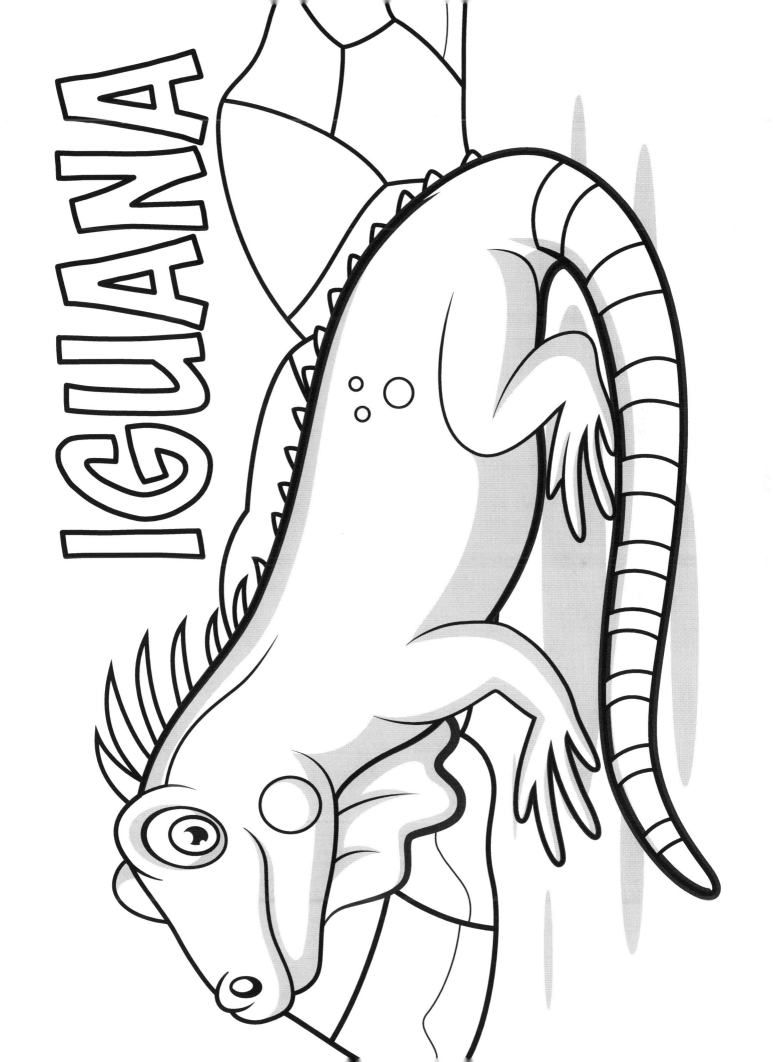

IGUANA

RABBIT

# PONY

SLEEPY SLOTH

# SEAL

# MONKEY

MIGHTY T-REX

GROOOAAA

!!!RRAAAAAA

# GOOSE

# GOAT

# DOLPHIN

# CAMEL

# FROG

# FISHING PENGUIN

# SQUIRREL

TURKEY

# WINTER WALRUS

OSTRICH

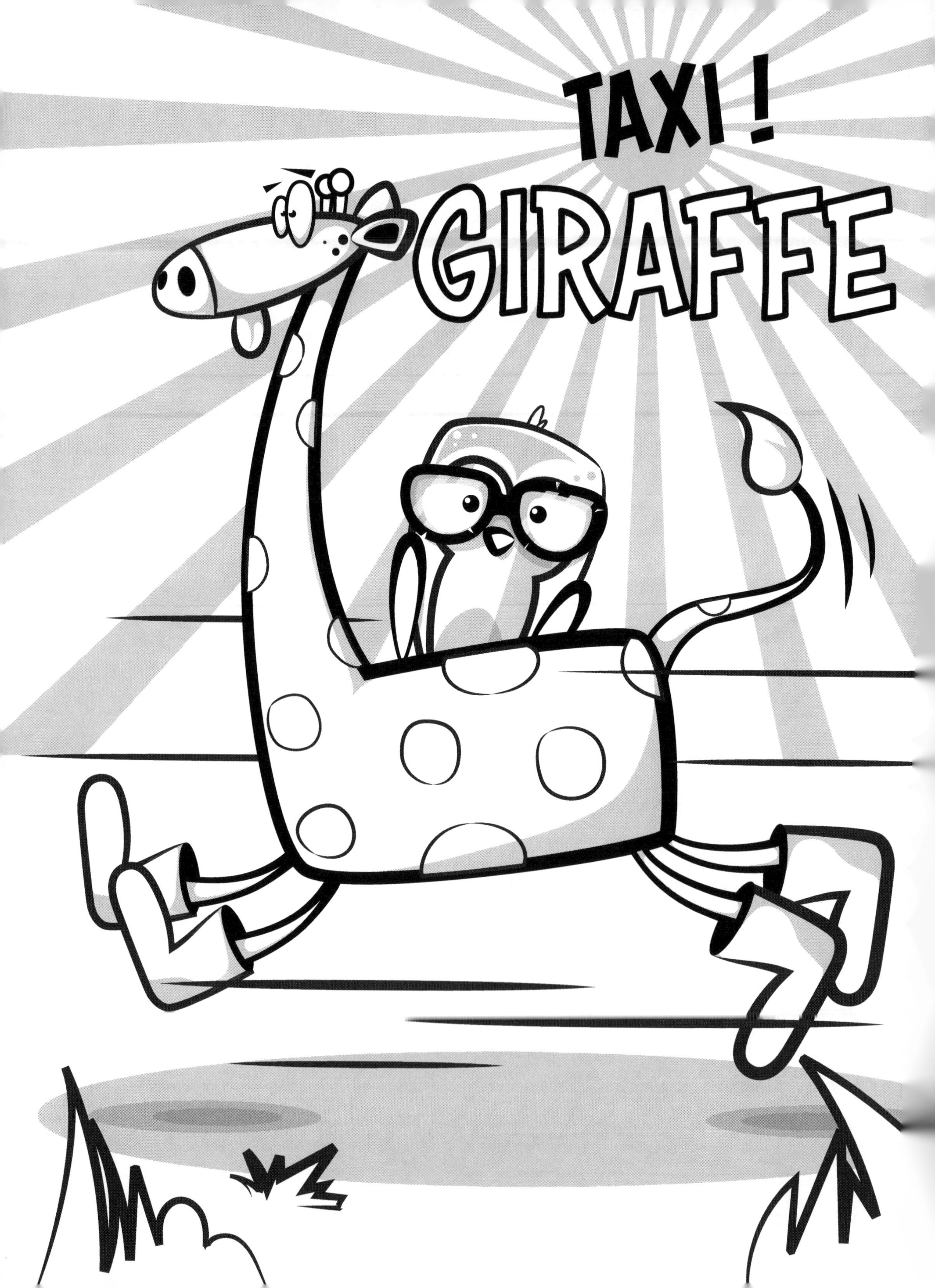
TAXI !
GIRAFFE

CROCODILE

CHIMPANZEE

# TURTLE

SHRIMP

# HUNGRY HAMSTER

# ZEBRA

# SWAN

ICE SKATING DEER

We hope you enjoyed this book. As we learn and grow, we'd love a rating or review for it on Amazon, if you have time. **Thank You!**

Loads more from Under The Cover Press

available at **amazon**

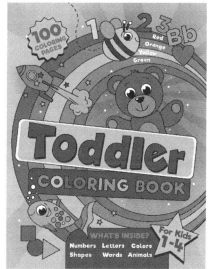

ISBN 979-8552067565

ISBN 979-8509492808

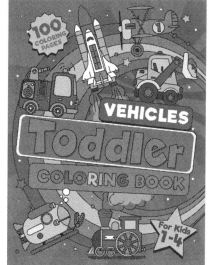

ISBN 979-8520557715

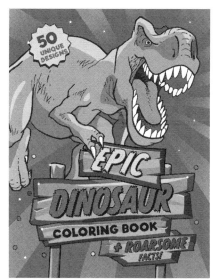

ISBN 979-8590346219

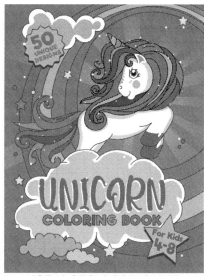

ISBN 979-8695161878

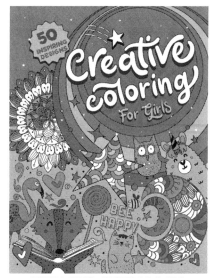

ISBN 979-8575406419

ISBN 979-8559845876

ISBN 979-8559850436

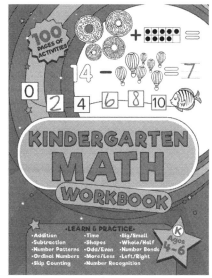

ISBN 979-8717778565

Made in the USA
Middletown, DE
09 March 2024

51126503R00060